# Breakthrough Book of Poems and Prayers

# BREAKTHROUGH BOOK OF POEMS AND PRAYERS

Felicia Edmond

AGD PUBLISHING

BREAKTHROUGH: A BOOK OF POEMS AND PRAYERS

Published by AGD Publishing Company

Copyright © 2020 by Felicia Edmond

All rights reserved.

No part of this book may be reproduced, distributed or transmitted in any form by any means, graphic, electronic, or mechanical, including photocopy, recording, taping, or by an information storage or retrieval system, without permission in writing from the publisher, except in the case of reprints in the content of reviews, quotes or references.

Unless otherwise noted, Scripture quotations are taken from the New King James Version of the Bible.

Printed in the United States of America

Paperback 978-1-7346758-5-6

eBook    978-1-7346758-6-3

# DEDICATION

*To all who need a breakthrough in any area of your life, this book is dedicated to You.*

*As you read the poems, prayers, and declarations, I pray that you break through to the other side of your situation by faith.*

*Jesus, the Christ, is the God of the breakthrough!*

# Contents

ACKNOWLEDGEMENTS xi
A TRIBUTE TO MY DAD xv

NEW LIFE 1

TOTAL SURRENDER 3

CHANGED FROM THE INSIDE OUT 7

LOVE OF GOD 9

ABBA 11

MY HEALER 13

CHILDHOOD TRAUMA 15

REJECTION 19

PUSHING THROUGH DEPRESSION 23

FORGIVENESS 27

WHEN NO ONE CLAPS 29

IDENTITY 31

THE REAL ME 33

HERE TO STAY 35

RESTORATION 37

BREAKING THROUGH INSECURITY 39

TRUE FREEDOM 41

PURPOSE 43

DESTINY 47

GOD OF INCREASE 49

A BLESSED MARRIAGE 51

INFERTILITY 53

OUR CHILDREN 55

A MOTHER'S PRAYER 57

THE BEAUTY OF FRIENDSHIPS 61

GOD'S GRACE 63

GOD'S PROMISES 65

NEVER GIVE UP 67

DREAM AGAIN 69

BREAKTHROUGH 71

*BIOGRAPHY 73*

# ACKNOWLEDGEMENTS

I thank my Lord and Savior Jesus Christ who is my life. For without You, I can do nothing. Thank You for being first in my life and loving me.

To my husband Jerry. You are my biggest support and you are God's expression of love in my life.

To my beautiful children Joelle and Jonathan. I love you and you are my support beyond what you can imagine. Dream Big!

In loving memory of my father Sherman Peterson. Your hard work and dedication to our family growing up was priceless; it is a huge part of who I am today.

To my loving mother Doris, I am forever grateful for all your sacrifices and love. I love you so much!

To my siblings Gordon, Darlene, and Theresa and their spouses. I love you all. We have always supported each other in a special way. You mean more to me than you will ever know.

To my beautiful mother- in- law Lois and my late father-in- law John T and to the family, I love you always.

My nieces and nephews, I love you. The best is yet to come!

To all my extended family, I love and pray for all!

To my sister friend of over 40 years, Christa; thank you for listening to my poems in the night hour and telling me not to give up.

To all that I call friends, my prayer partner, my covenant sisters, and God's Daughters of Transparency, I love you all.

To my Pastors and church family, thank you for giving me accountability to not only be a hearer of the Word but also a doer of the Word.

To all my spiritual midwives, coaches, and mentors down through the years; thank you for helping me birth out the vision of God on the inside.

To a special mentor, Pastor Sonja Mahoney. Thank you

for allowing God to use you to call out the gifts and treasures buried deep within me during a difficult time.

Thank you so much to Allison G. Daniels for coaching me in God's purpose and her publishing staff for helping me to bring this book to fruition.

A special thanks to my photographer Shannon Bland.

I want to thank Tonya Overton and her Ministry Family for encouraging me to live and dream as a new creation in Christ.

# A TRIBUTE TO MY DAD

It has been many years since you went home,

I pray you are meeting with Him at the throne.

You were a man of sacrifice and in your own way a man of love,

Your love came straight from Heaven above.

You were smart and I saw you as of the genius class.

If you had the opportunity, perhaps your career pursuit would have been math.

You were quiet but were of tremendous strength,

I only had nineteen years with you,

But truly I cannot measure the time length.

All the hours you worked, moving your family to a blessed place.

## Felicia Edmond

Every sacrifice you made

Was a treasure embraced.

You did not express it with much affection or words,

But when I look back in time, your love was clearly heard.

Your last words to me were, "Do not let anyone tell you what you cannot do."

I can now live out those words –in clear view.

Your legacy was both determination and perseverance, but clearly motivated by love.

I hope you are now enjoying Heaven above.

All My Love, Felicia

# NEW LIFE

My life was filled with darkness and sin,
And then Jesus, You stepped in.
I became new; I was filled with Your light,
Realizing You had won the fight.
A new song in my heart, I now rejoice,
I made You my choice.
I no longer face life alone,
Even with the struggles, You are right there on the throne.
My life will never be the same,
I have hope, I have love, I have Your Name.
You have seated me in Heavenly places,
And I can now come boldly to the throne of grace.
It is by grace I have been saved through faith in You,
You are, forever, in my heart and my life is made new!

**PRAYER:** Heavenly Father, please come into my heart right now. I turn from a life of sin. I accept Jesus as my

Lord and Savior and yes, I believe that You raised Jesus from the dead. I thank You Father for my new life in Christ Jesus. In Jesus' Name, Amen!

**DECLARATION:** I am saved. I am born again, and my past is over. I am no longer in darkness, but I walk in His marvelous light. I am a new creation and I have new life.

*"...that if you confess with your mouth the Lord Jesus and believe in your heart that God has raised Him from the dead, you will be saved."* Romans 10:9

**REFLECTIONS:**

_____
_____
_____
_____
_____
_____
_____
_____
_____

# TOTAL SURRENDER

I surrender and fully commit my life
As I meditate on Your Word day and night.
Great is Your faithfulness as Your mercies are new every morning.
You fill my life as I embrace this journey
I give my all to You Lord
I desire to live by Your Word
Every step –every day
I commit to Your way.
Order my steps and be my guide,
It is myself that I must deny.
You said "Deny myself take up my cross and follow You"
You Dear Lord are the one I pursue.
I know as I surrender to You, I can't go wrong,
To You, every day I desire to belong. Every day it is for

You that I long
I realize that Your presence is always here,
You never leave me nor forsake me,
I put my total trust in You, and I stay near
I totally surrender to You, and I enjoy
Your embrace,
Every day I am fulfilled, as I seek Your face.

PRAYER: Heavenly Father, I thank You that I have totally surrendered my life to You. I commit every area of my life to you. I realize that my life is not my own. I give You every care and every struggle. Lord I trust You and rely on You. You are the only one that can help me break through. I thank You for leading me and guiding me in the name of Jesus, I pray. Amen!

DECLARATION: My life belongs to Jesus. I surrender to Him. I cast every care on Him because He cares for me.

*"...casting all your care upon Him, for He cares for you."* 1 Peter 5:7

## REFLECTIONS:

# CHANGED FROM THE INSIDE OUT

It's in Jesus Christ, I am now free,
Because where the Spirit of the Lord is, there is liberty.
I now go from glory to glory,
I am changed into Your image.
Beholding You, Lord,
I meditate on Your Word and Your Word is my sword.
Old things have passed away,
I am made new…
New, in Christ.
He gave me abundant life.
So I sit and rest in all He has for me,
Because in Him, I am completely free.
Who the Son has made free, is truly free indeed.

**PRAYER:** Heavenly Father, I thank You and worship You. Thank You for true freedom. Father help me to receive the change You placed on the inside of me.

Help me, Dear Lord to come to You and experience all that You have for me. In Jesus' Name, Amen!

**DECLARATION:** I am new in Christ. There is nothing holding me back. I am changed from the inside out.

*"But we all, with unveiled face, beholding as in a mirror the glory of the Lord, are being transformed into the same image from glory to glory, just as by the Spirit of the Lord."* 2 Corinthians 3:18

**REFLECTIONS:**

_____
_____
_____
_____
_____
_____
_____

# LOVE OF GOD

Love of God,
Pour like never before
Jesus it is You, I adore.
Your unconditional love surrounds me
On every side,
It's in Your love that I abide.
In times of trials and tribulations, I find peace,
Your love brings me triumph and comfort through grief.
Your love brings me safety and ease,
Even through troubles, Your love does not cease.
Perfect love of God, surround me and cast out my fears,
Your love makes me draw near.
Through Your love I am healed, I am delivered and made whole.
Your love brings me through every season,
And gives me Your sweet presence to behold.

**PRAYER:** Heavenly Father –My Abba Father, I thank You for Your unconditional love. Help me, please to receive that love that only You can give. Help me to know You fully through Your love. Help me to focus on Your love. Take away all fear as I embrace Your love. You have not given me the spirit of fear, but of power, love, and a sound mind. In Jesus' name, Amen!

**DECLARATION:** I am loved by God. His perfect love casts out every fear in my life. I speak His Word continually as I draw near to Jesus. I walk in faith and not fear. I am comforted. I am whole. I walk in love.

*"For God has not given us a spirit of fear, but of power and of love and of a sound mind."* 2 Timothy 1:7

**REFLECTIONS:**

_____
_____
_____
_____
_____
_____
_____
_____
_____
_____

# ABBA

You are my Father
My true Dad.
I need You so much.
You fill the void,
You give me joy.
It is because of You, my heart sings,
It is because of You that my eyes are now open,
By faith I can now clearly see,
Destiny, faith, light and Agape' love,
From the glorious Heaven above.
But You also live on the inside of me,
Through Your amazing love, I have peace and victory.
Nothing can separate Your love from me,
It is only because of You, I believe
I walk in Your power, grace and glory,
So, Abba, Father, You mean the world to me.
Yes, I am the King's daughter,
You truly bring out the princess in me.

**PRAYER:** Heavenly Father, I thank You that I can call You Abba Father. I thank You that I have been brought near to You by the blood of Jesus Christ. Please help me to continue to draw near to You in my relationship with You. Thank You for adopting me as Your child. I receive Your love and I love You with all my heart, in Jesus' name. Amen!

**DECLARATION:** God is my Abba Father. I depend and lean on Him. I am close to my Father and I will stay in His presence.

*"For you did not receive the spirit of bondage again to fear, but you received the Spirit of adoption by whom we cry out, "Abba, Father."* Romans 8:15

**REFLECTIONS:**

_____
_____
_____
_____
_____
_____
_____
_____

# MY HEALER

Christ, You are King,
In You I have everything.
Like the woman in the Bible with the issue of blood ...
I am healed ... and Your power is revealed.
You give sight to the blind,
And in You only true deliverance we can find.
Only in You, miracles come through.
You raise the dead,
You give us life,
It is with our faith in You that we can fight.
You see we fight the good fight of faith,
But because of You, we always win,
We even have victory over sin.
So, dear friends in Christ, you may ask when do I receive my healing?
It was accomplished on the cross,
When He saved us from being lost.
When He died He gave us all things,

Our healing, our justification, our peace within.
The wait has ended,
Just rest in Him and surrender, as you win.

**PRAYER:** Heavenly Father, thank You for my healing. Please help me to receive the manifestation of my healing because it is by Your stripes that I am healed. I thank You Lord that You forgive every one of my sins; You healed all my diseases according to Your Word. So, thank You, Lord, for being my Jehovah Rapha, my Healer. In Jesus' name I pray, Amen!

**DECLARATION:** I am the healed of the Lord. I walk in my healing. I walk in divine health, even as I wait for the full manifestation; I will never forget Your benefits, Dear Lord. Healing belongs to me, now!

*"But He was wounded for our transgressions, He was bruised for our iniquities; The chastisement for our peace was upon Him, And by His stripes we are healed."* Isaiah 53:5

**REFLECTIONS:**

_____
_____
_____
_____
_____

# CHILDHOOD TRAUMA

Childhood trauma... childhood trauma!
You have no pull on me.
Because in Christ I have the victory.
He gave me my identity.
Yes, *before* Christ, you did exist but now in Him, I persist.
At one time I lost my voice,
But in Him now, I can rejoice.
Praise is where I release,
It is where I find peace.
Because the Healer lives in me.
So, trauma, I come face to face, and I look you in the eye.
You see, I am no longer afraid,
Because every day is a new day.
For my healing to take place,

You see, it has already taken place on Calvary.
Every day I die daily, and I remind myself that the cross and His resurrection lives in me.

PRAYER: Heavenly Father I worship You and thank You that You knew me before I was in my mother's womb. Please help me to receive the healing You have for me for all passed trauma. Help me to forgive all who have hurt me, and to forgive myself. Help me to walk in Your love and freedom. Help me to experience Your presence because You are close to the brokenhearted. I receive my emotional healing now. It is by Your stripes that I am healed. In Jesus' name, Amen!

DECLARATION: My past no longer holds me in bondage. I am a new creation in Christ Jesus. I am rooted and established in Christ's love and I know the fullness of His love. I worship and praise God.

*"Therefore, if anyone is in Christ, he is a new creation; old things have passed away; behold, all things have become new."* 2 Corinthians 5:17

## REFLECTIONS:

# REJECTION

Rejection, rejection I am talking to you.
You have no clue,
That you have no power over me,
Because the lover of my soul made me free.
It is in this freedom where I have found my identity.
My identity says I am loved by God and I am accepted in the beloved.
So, you see –I am loved.
So, rejection, every time you try to appear.
You must realize that because of the blood of Jesus, my life's been purchased and bought near and dear –to Him.
Every wall must come down.
Because healing has truly been found.
Rejection, you must go whether perceived or real — no matter how I feel.
Feelings come and they go.
And this I do know.

That the love of Jesus is eternal, it's perfect and its truth.
All things have truly been made anew.
So, rejection, you must go; as a matter of fact you are now gone,
Because my relationship with Christ shines, and it lives on.

**PRAYER**: Heavenly Father, I thank You that You never leave me nor forsake me. Thank You Father for Your unconditional love. I thank You that You have chosen me in You before the foundation of the world. I thank You that I am accepted in the beloved. I thank You that I call You Abba, Father. Help me Father to fully walk in Your love and acceptance. Father, I embrace Your love right now and it covers every area of my life. In Jesus' name. Amen!

**DECLARATION**: I am accepted in the beloved. I am loved. I am God's beloved child. He is always with me. I am chosen by God.

*"...to the praise of the glory of His grace, by which He made us accepted in the Beloved."* Ephesians 1:6

## REFLECTIONS:

_____
_____
_____
_____
_____
_____
_____
_____
_____
_____

# PUSHING THROUGH DEPRESSION

I learned that being in despair is not my friend,
One day my precious daughter stepped in,
And said to me no more! And then I realized again that it is God who opens doors.
I do not have to fret.
I do not have to fear,
I am His child and to Him I draw near.
Nearer to the cross and with resurrection power I see,
I see all that Christ has for me.
As I renew my mind on His Word,
I will always forever push forward.
I am no longer stuck.
I stand, I look, and I see over the horizon,
I can see my mourning turned into dancing,

I see my joy, gladness, and my peace,
Because of and by His love, it is now a reality
So, depression you are gone,
Because God says for me to "Arise and shine for your light has come".
The glory of the Lord rises upon me,
You see His glory is all over me,
And there is an abundance of love overflowing to set others free.

**PRAYER:** Heavenly Father, thank You Lord for helping me overcome depression as I meditate on Your Word and worship You daily. I thank You Lord that my confidence is in You. I thank You that You have given me the garment of praise for the spirit of heaviness. I thank You Lord that I have the fullness of joy in Your presence. Help me to experience that joy each and every day, in Jesus' name. Amen!

**DECLARATION:** I am full of joy. I am no longer stuck in depression or any other bondage. I am moving forward in all that God has for me. I praise God and I experience His presence daily.

*"You have turned for me my mourning into dancing; You have put off [a]my sackcloth and clothed me with gladness,"* Psalm 30:11

REFLECTIONS:

# FORGIVENESS

I have been broken hearted and betrayed in life,
And sometimes, quite a bit of conflicts and strife,
But then, I remember, I belong to the Great Physician, the Healer.
He heals my broken heart,
And He alone, gives me a new start.
So, I must forgive,
I must let go,
You see, Christ has forgiven me, this I know,
Total and complete forgiveness brings freedom and love,
I cast my cares on Him and let the anointing flow.
I worship Him and receive His kindness towards me,
Because now I can clearly see, that
When I let go and truly forgive,
The battle belongs to Him and
Clearly, the victory belongs to me.

**PRAYER:** Heavenly Father, help me to forgive others and myself by faith. As Christ has forgiven me, I must always forgive. Please heal the hurt that I have experienced Lord, as only You can do. It is by Your stripes that I am healed. I fully forgive and release others and I am set free in Jesus' name, I pray. Amen!

**DECLARATION:** I forgive those who hurt me. I release them and I release myself. I walk in total freedom and in the love of God.

*"[b]earing with one another, and forgiving one another, if anyone has a complaint against another; even as Christ forgave you, so you also must do."* Colossians 3:13

**REFLECTIONS:**

_____
_____
_____
_____
_____
_____
_____
_____
_____

# WHEN NO ONE CLAPS

I shared, I performed, I spoke,
And I thought I did my best,
But no one clapped for me,
I asked, "Did I fail, or do I have the victory?"
The Father says you must realize you pleased me.
You see, I am the one who receives the glory.
Jesus is Lord over your life, and I have written your story.
Why are you cast down and why are you discouraged?
Be strong in me and have courage.
How you live and all you do is for me,
When you magnify me in your life, you will see,
If no one claps for you, you still succeed,
You must remember your audience is Me.

PRAYER: Heavenly Father I thank You that You are my confidence. You are the one who affirms me and loves me. Father I glorify You in my life. If God be for me, who can be against me. You are the one who justifies me because You have chosen me before the foundation of the world. I thank You Lord that You are working in me and through me in the name of Jesus I pray, Amen!

**DECLARATION:** I am approved by God. I work as unto the Lord as He has created me to do. My total acceptance is in Christ.

*"And whatever you do, do it heartily, as to the Lord and not to men,* Colossians 3:23

**REFLECTIONS:**

_____
_____
_____
_____
_____
_____
_____
_____
_____

# IDENTITY

Who am I, I may ask,
It is in His presence that I bask
That's where I get the answers to the questions I ask.
He says to me, you are who I made you to be.
You are loved and
You are set free
Because you believe in me.
You are the apple of my eye
You are my beloved
I placed your tears in a bottle and I hear your cry.
Your identity is that you belong to me.
When I look at you, I see the image of me.
You are made in my image
You are my friend
You are special and dear to me
That is your identity.
You'll never have to question again
Because in me it is where it all began.

It is in me that you live move and have your being,
And ...now that you know your true identity,
You'll be my vessel, so that others may become free.

**PRAYER:** Heavenly Father my identity is found in You alone. You have created me and saved me because of Your love and grace. I thank You Lord that I am special to You and I can rest in knowing that nothing can separate me from Your love, in Jesus' name I pray. Amen!

**DECLARATION:** My identity is found in Christ. Christ died for me and His resurrection power lives on the inside of me. I am complete in Him.

*"So God created man in His own image; in the image of God He created him; male and female He created them."* Genesis 1:27

**REFLECTIONS:**

_____
_____
_____
_____
_____
_____
_____

# THE REAL ME

I was hidden for a long time and I wore a mask,
Because I did not think I was up to the task.
On some occasions, I even lost my voice,
Because I myself made a choice.
To sit back in silence and let others determine my path,
Until one day Christ called me to arise,
And each day I began taking off the mask.
He said to me, "Daughter, as you hear my voice, you use your voice."
You my child, answer my call,
I will hold you up in me, you will not fall.
Through Christ, the real me is revealed,
And I am emotionally and lovingly healed.
As Christ unlocks my gifts, my talents, and my skills,
To bless others – and because I am in Him, I am sealed.
In Him is now the only place I hide,
In Him I will forever abide,

As the real me is revealed from the inside,
And now on the outside His light truly shines.

**PRAYER:** Heavenly Father I call forth my emotional healing and I come against all fear. Father help me to truly release myself to You. I thank You that I do not have to hide because You are truly the One who lives on the inside. You are the one who works in me both to will and to do for Your good pleasure. I thank You Lord that I am who I am by Your grace, in Jesus' name. Amen!

**DECLARATION:** I no longer hide. Christ's purpose is birthed in me. I am healed and I now live for Him.

*"[j]ust as He chose us in Him before the foundation of the world, that we should be holy and without blame before Him in love,"* Ephesians 1:4

**REFLECTIONS:**

_____
_____
_____
_____
_____
_____
_____

# HERE TO STAY

I am here to stay.
I was born, for such a time as this,
And my destiny will not be missed.
There is an assignment that only I can do,
So, I must persevere and push right on through.
I will make it through, to the other side,
I surrender to God and I will no longer hide.
There are lives that only I can touch,
Because of His love, He has given me so much.
I am loved. I am healed. I am fulfilled,
To the Holy Spirit I do yield.
So, I rest in His love and now I am complete.
And I no longer compete, because you see, in Him I am unique.
He knew me before I was in my mother's womb,
He called me. He ordained me. I am His workmanship, and that is the truth.
So, I stand in this truth and boldly proclaim,

That His Kingdom purpose for me will be obtained. I am here to stay to accomplish His will and to walk in His ways.

**PRAYER:** Heavenly Father –My Abba Father, I thank You for creating me with a purpose. Please help me to never lose heart and to always focus on Your love and what You have for me. You said in Your Word that You know the plans for me; plans to prosper me and not to harm me; plans to give me a future and a hope. Help me to walk in this truth. In Jesus' name, Amen!

**DECLARATION:** I am fearfully and wonderfully made by God. I have a purpose in Him. I have a great future in Him. I walk in the plans He has for me. He is using me for His Kingdom purposes.

*"I will praise You, for I am fearfully and wonderfully made; Marvelous are Your works, And that my soul knows very well."* Psalm 139:14

**REFLECTIONS:**

_____
_____
_____
_____
_____

# RESTORATION

I thought it was hopeless
And all I could see was the end,
But then God's restoration quickly stepped in.
He said I will restore the many years
Those times when all you could see were tears.
God said, "I am pouring my anointing upon you
And then I say "Live!"
There is more, the best is yet to come,
It is like your journey has just begun.
So, you, do not look back in despair,
Realize that your hope is near.
Have faith in me, and you will see,
I am a rewarder of those who diligently seek me.
So, I say Lord I would have fainted had
I not believed I would see Your goodness for me
Lord I believe! All is restored,
First my peace, my hope, and my faith in Your Word!
Sweet manifestations are now my sweet reward!

**PRAYER**: Heavenly Father I thank You for restoration. I thank You Lord that I can begin again. Thank You for restoring me after all the years of pain. Thank You Lord that I now embrace the new. I forget what is behind and I look forward to the future that You have for me. I thank You Lord that with You all things are possible and for my shame You give me double, in Jesus' name. Amen!

**DECLARATION**: Years have been restored to my life. I am moving forward. I am excited about the new!

*"So I will restore to you the years that the swarming locust has eaten, The crawling locust, The consuming locust, And the chewing locust, My great army which I sent among you."* Joel 2:25

**REFLECTIONS:**

_____
_____
_____
_____
_____
_____
_____
_____
_____

# BREAKING THROUGH INSECURITY

**B**reaking through the pain,
With Christ I have many blessings to gain.
He loves me,
He qualified me,
He called me.
So, I focus in on His Voice,
This is my choice.
No matter what has happened in the past,
I press toward the mark of the high calling in Christ,
Because my purpose in Him will last.
I hold fast to the liberty for which Christ has made me free,
There are no more insecurities, no more low self esteem,

No more bondage,
I have a strong, everlasting victory.
I focus on Him in all that I say and all that I do,
Yes, Praise Jesus, I am ready and excited for the new.

**PRAYER:** Dear Heavenly Father, help me to realize that I am already victorious in You. Help me to realize the truth that I am secure and free in You. Thank You Lord that You have great plans for me, and You are using me to Your glory. Thank You Lord that I am accepted and chosen in the beloved and by You. In Jesus' name, Amen!

**DECLARATION:** Through Christ Jesus, I am confident. I am secure. I bear great fruit. I am bold as a lion because I am victorious in Him.

*"Therefore if the Son makes you free, you shall be free indeed..."* John 8:36

**REFLECTIONS:**

_____
_____
_____
_____
_____
_____

# TRUE FREEDOM

True freedom is found in God's Word
Oh, by the way, have you not heard,
That the truth will make you free,
Freedom and deliverance are your profound destiny.
So, I ask you, what do you need to be freed from?
Unbelief, low self esteem, addictions...
Maybe so much more.
But, with an awareness of your freedom,
You will soar.
The truth is that you are already free
You see, it is finished,
Because of the Good News established
at the cross.
So, I share with you, let go of the bondage, release the chains and let go of the loss.
Your battle is already won!
Sound the alarm!
As you renew your mind to the victory that is already

yours,
With His resurrection, He has won the war!

**PRAYER:** Heavenly Father please help me to experience the freedom that You have already accomplished on the cross for me. Whom the Son has set free, is free indeed. Help me to experience Your freedom as I experience Your Word and Your presence. Where the Spirit of the Lord is – truly, there is liberty. In Jesus' name, Amen!

**DECLARATION:** I am free in Christ. I am free from every addiction and bondage. I have my true freedom now in the name of Jesus.

*"Now the Lord is the Spirit; and where the Spirit of the Lord is, there is liberty."* 2 Corinthians 3:17

**REFLECTIONS:**

_____
_____
_____
_____
_____
_____
_____
_____

# PURPOSE

God You have an amazing purpose and plan for me,
In You I have great clarity.
I see all that You have designed for me.
I belong to You.
I am free in You.
As a matter of fact, I am Your masterpiece.
You took the time to create me,
Fearfully and wonderfully –You made me.
With the price You paid…
At the cross for me.
I have gifts! I have talents! You called me! I have sweet victory!
So, I write the vision down,
I am making it plain,
I am healed from all pain.
Because You have breathed new life in me,
To be used as your vessel,

For someone else's deliverance and destiny.
Yes, You have an amazing plan and purpose for me Magnificent Lord now let it unfold.

PRAYER: Heavenly Father, I thank You and I am excited for all that You have planned for me. Help me to follow Your beautiful plan and vision for my life. Help me to continue in this plan no matter what obstacles I face. By faith, I believe that Your plan will unfold, in Jesus' name. Now unto Him, who is able to do exceedingly, and abundantly, above all that I can ask or think according to the power that works in me. In Jesus' name, I pray. Amen!

DECLARATION: God loves me. God uses me to glorify His name concerning the lives of others. His purpose for me is amazing and I walk in His purpose for me.

*"For we are His workmanship, created in Christ Jesus for good works, which God prepared beforehand that we should walk in them."* Ephesians 2:10

## REFLECTIONS:

# DESTINY

I now have a delightful destiny,
Look at what God has for me.
The enemy told me it was over and there was no purpose, no
plan for me.
Why are you on earth, he asked me?
I answered and said because I have a destiny.
Way beyond what you can see.
It not only leads to my victory but also, to others' victories.
Why, because my Redeemer lives within me.

**PRAYER**: Heavenly Father, help me to bask in Your presence and draw near to You. As I draw near to You, precious Lord, You, are drawing near to me. Thank You Lord for speaking to me and revealing Yourself to me. It is during these times that You reveal Your great plans for me. In Jesus' name. Amen!

**DECLARATION:** I am a child of God. I draw near to God and I seek God's face. God, You do have an amazing plan for me. I am not forgotten; I am born for such a time as this.

*"For I know the thoughts that I think toward you, says the Lord, thoughts of peace and not of evil, to give you a future and a hope."* Jeremiah 29:11

**REFLECTIONS:**

_____
_____
_____
_____
_____
_____
_____
_____
_____
_____

# GOD OF INCREASE

Jesus, You are the God of increase,
In You, all lack will cease.
It's only in You that we have the best,
Even here on the earth, we can enter unto Your rest.
Because promotion does not come from the east, west, north or the south.
Promotion is found in the Lord,
It is in You that we can victoriously move forward.
It's in You that we live, move, and have our being,
So we must give You all the glory and Your praises we must sing.
So why should we doubt, why should we fear,
Because with You, the "suddenly" will appear.
So thank You Lord, for our increase,
With You there's nothing missing, nothing broken and

nothing lacking...
We have peace.

**PRAYER:** Heavenly Father, I thank You Lord for being Jehovah Jireh, My Provider. Please help me to focus on You as my source, as my only source. Thank You for supplying all my need, according to Your riches in glory in Christ Jesus. I thank You Lord that You delight in my prosperity as I am Your servant. Lord, for Your Word says, do not worry about tomorrow, for tomorrow will take care of itself. I will continuously seek You my God. In Jesus' name I pray, Amen!

**DECLARATION:** I am prosperous in Christ. I am promoted in Christ. I do not worry, and I do not fear. All my needs are met in Christ. In fact, I have an overflow to give to others.

*"For exaltation comes neither from the east Nor from the west nor from the south."* Psalm 75:6

**REFLECTIONS:**

_____
_____
_____
_____
_____

# A BLESSED MARRIAGE

We leave, we cleave, and we cling to one another,
So shall the two become one.
A new life together, we have begun.
We submit ourselves to God and each other.
It is in Him that we live, we move, and we have our being,
As a three-strand chord,
Together we diligently seek Him and have our reward.
We thank Him for His great plan,
For a future and a blessed hope.
Through His love we become close.
Although we may have struggles to overcome,
We pray, we persevere, and we remember, we are one.
Each day gets brighter and each season gets better,

Our love is exciting; it is an adventure and on earth, it is forever.

PRAYER: Heavenly Father, thank You for blessing our marriage. Help us to submit to You Lord and rely on You. Help us to make You the center of our marriage as we love and forgive one another. Help us to realize we are not alone but You are with us. You will never leave us nor forsake us. Thank You for blessing us with abundant lives in our marriage, in Jesus' name. Amen.

DECLARATION: Our marriage is blessed. We show the love of Christ in our marriage. We seek God together and we are close to one another. We are excited about all that the Lord is doing in our marriage.

*"For this reason a man shall leave his father and mother and be joined to his wife, and the two shall become one flesh."* Ephesians 5:31

REFLECTIONS:

_____
_____
_____
_____
_____
_____

# INFERTILITY

Infertility, infertility you are defeated and you cannot stay around,
You see, in Jesus is where my peace is found.
Peace represents wholeness and this I know to be true,
So, you cannot stay here and think you'll make me blue.
Because I have had many sad days hanging around you,
Until I learned my God's truth.
It is finished! Christ died for me and His resurrection power lives in me.
And with His power comes victory.
He did it for Sarah, He did it for Hannah and He did it for Elizabeth.
And I know He'll do the same for me.
Wait a minute – in truth and it is a fact, it's already done for me.
It will manifest itself in victory.
So, infertility you have to go because my

healing has already taken place.
In Jesus' name, in every area, I win the race.

**PRAYER:** Heavenly Father You said in Your Word that You place the barren woman in a home and that You will make her a mother. You said that I am a fruitful vine in my husband's home. So, Father, I thank You that by faith, I am no longer barren and I can and I will experience the joy of motherhood. In Jesus' name I pray, Amen!

**DECLARATION:** By faith I stand on the Word of God. God is my healer. I am a mother because of Him. This too shall come to pass.

*"He grants the [a]barren woman a home, Like a joyful mother of children."* Psalm 113:9

**REFLECTIONS:**

_____
_____
_____
_____
_____
_____
_____

# OUR CHILDREN

Our children are gifts and they are His reward,
That God entrusted to us.
We dedicate them to Christ.
As we train them up in Him and help shape their lives.
We teach them that they have greatness and
purpose in You, Dear Lord,
To live the abundant life and always in You move forward.
So, we say to them, remember God's Word and the gifts He placed on the inside,
To make a difference, as He is your guide.
You are precious to us and we love you beyond
what you can see,
As we have directed you, to catapult you into your destiny.
Remember that all His promises are yes and Amen,

Jesus is your Lord and never forget He is your constant companion, your constant friend.

PRAYER: Heavenly Father thank You for the gift of our children. Please help us as we train them and teach them. Help them to draw near to You in their relationship with You. Guide them in every step of their lives. I thank You Lord for loving and protecting our children. I thank You that the seed of the righteous is delivered and great is the peace of our children. Thank You for blessing our children in the name of Jesus, I pray. Amen!

DECLARATION: Our children are blessed and highly favored of the Lord. They have a wonderful relationship with Him. They have a great destiny in Christ. Nothing hinders the destiny of our children.

*"Behold, children are a heritage from the Lord, The fruit of the womb is a reward."* Psalm 127:3

REFLECTIONS:

_____

_____

_____

_____

_____

# A MOTHER'S PRAYER

We love, we nurture, we hold,
We hold our children close.
As they grow up, we realize we must give God control.
As they encounter the trials and tribulations in life
We may feel our hands are tied
Then we clearly see the Lord is truly on our side
We no longer need to worry or doubt
Because of our prayer requests, we see the mountains moved
And we see the will of God come about
We see that the seed of the righteous is always delivered
And great is our children's peace
We continue to stand in prayer, and we feel and experience the release
We never give up because our prayers release Heaven

to earth
We see God's desires for our children are birthed.
We know that there is nothing like a mother's prayer
It changes the atmosphere as we lay it all at His feet,
Our children overcome, always triumph and will never be in defeat.

**PRAYER:** Heavenly Father I thank You for our children. I thank You that no matter what the current circumstances, they can change. I thank You Lord that I put my total trust in You regarding our children. I thank You that my prayers are working in the lives of our children. As I pray Your promises over our children, Your Word will not come back void. Thank you, Lord, in Jesus' name I pray. Amen!

**DECLARATION:** Our prayers are working. Our children are blessed. Our children are in the will of God. Our children are successful, purposeful, and delivered.

*"Confess your trespasses to one another, and pray for one another, that you may be healed. The effective, fervent prayer of a righteous man avails much."* James 5:16

## REFLECTIONS:

_____
_____
_____
_____
_____
_____
_____
_____
_____
_____

# THE BEAUTY OF FRIENDSHIPS

God gives me the beauty of friendships,
Friendships bless me in all seasons of life,
We care for one another and we even overcome strife.
Friends are there in both the dark times and seasons of delight,
We share wisdom, we grow together, and we share great insight.
We are transparent, authentic and we show the love of Christ
Friends help us to dream and to hold on to our faith,
Our friendships in Christ give us a place to feel safe,
We pray for one another and we share in His grace.
I praise God for every friendship, which is so unique,
Each friend has a purpose in my life and in God I seek.
I do pray for the right friendships, that they are ordained by Christ,

And that God blesses me to be used in each friend's life.

I praise God for my friendships, as we sharpen one another,

As we enter our next level of glory, in Christ, with each other.

**PRAYER:** Heavenly Father, I thank You Lord for being my best friend. You are a friend that sticks closer than a brother. Heavenly Father, please give me the friendships that are a reflection of You, and help me likewise, to be that friend to others. I thank You Lord for sincere friendships in You, in Jesus' name. Amen!

**DECLARATION:** Jesus is my best friend. I have friendships sent from God. Through Christ, I am a godly friend to others.

*"As iron sharpens iron, So a man sharpens the countenance of his friend."* Proverbs 27:17

**REFLECTIONS:**

_____
_____
_____
_____
_____

# GOD'S GRACE

I was filled with burdens
And encountering much shame,
Until my life was filled with pain.
I was losing the fight.
When I realized His yolk is easy and His burden is light.
Is when He said to me, "If I come to Him, He would give me rest."
No matter the storm and even through trials and tests.
Through faith, I must partake in His grace.
Through every trial that I face,
I must give Him my burdens and run this race.
And surrender fully to Him,
With complete commitment to His ways I begin
So, I no longer fight in my own strength
I give every battle over to Him.
The Word is my weapon and faith is my shield
With God as my Banner, the many victories I will surely win.

**PRAYER:** Heavenly Father, I need Your amazing grace. I surrender my will to You. Lord I give You every battle I face. Strengthen me in Your Word, that I may win the race. In Jesus' name I pray, Amen!

**DECLARATION:** I surrender to Christ. I commit to His ways. I receive His amazing grace.

*"Come to Me, all you who labor and are heavy laden, and I will give you rest. Take My yoke upon you and learn from Me, for I am gentle and lowly in heart, and you will find rest for your souls."* Matthew 11:28-29

**REFLECTIONS:**

_____
_____
_____
_____
_____
_____
_____
_____
_____

# GOD'S PROMISES

His promises belong to me
He meets my every need.
His Word is final, His Word is true
I continually meditate on His Word,
So that it can continually take root.
I am not discouraged, and I hold on to my faith,
I receive every promise by His grace.
Although my situation may look one way
I must remember what God's Word say.
Even if all I see is pain
God pours out His truth continually, like rain.
His truth is more real to me than what I see,
I know deep down inside what His Word has given me.
So, no matter what the situation
No matter the shame,
His faithful Word comes through
Because He magnifies His Word above all His name.

**PRAYER:** Heavenly Father I thank You that You are faithful to keep Your promises. Please help me to continue standing on Your Word. Help me to walk by faith and not by sight as I focus on You, in Jesus' name. Amen!

**DECLARATION:** God's Word is true. His promises are manifesting in my life. I have miracles working in my life.

*"For all the promises of God in Him are Yes, and in Him Amen, to the glory of God through us."* 2 Corinthians 1:20

**REFLECTIONS:**

_____
_____
_____
_____
_____
_____
_____
_____
_____
_____

# NEVER GIVE UP

Never give up!
In your heart you must say, continually, that God has precious
promises for me.
Because it's in Jesus Christ you see,
That you have an everlasting victory.
No matter what has come against you,
Keep moving, keep pushing, keep going.
Forget those things which are behind,
Press into your season and remember, it's your time.
You see, He knew you before the foundation of the world.
Only He will establish your future and your worth.
Because He delights in blessing you here on the earth.
Yes, He ordained you, sustains you and He called you,
Fulfill your calling and know His truth.
You are not forgotten, and you are not overlooked,
The best is yet to come so know you will have a new

outlook.
Now behold His Word and find the truth again,
And remember it is only on Him that you can depend.
So, Never Give Up!

PRAYER: I thank You Father that I am never forgotten or overlooked. I thank You that You have chosen and ordained me. Father help me to walk in the truth of Your Word as You use me for Your Glory. Thank You, Lord, that You never give up on me. In Jesus' name, Amen!

DECLARATION: I will never give up. I walk in the purpose God has for me. I rely on the promises of God for my life.

*"I press toward the goal for the prize of the upward call of God in Christ Jesus."* Philippians 3:14

REFLECTIONS:

_____
_____
_____
_____
_____
_____
_____
_____

# DREAM AGAIN

You thought your dreams had died,
But I ask you, "What did God put in you on the inside?"
New insight, ideas and His plans,
Your territory will expand.
As you delight yourself in Him and heed to His Word,
You can persevere, and you can push forward.
His miraculous power lives in you.
With His power abiding in you, and you continue to abide in Him,
You will bear much fruit.
Hold on to His promises,
Hold on to His truth
Walk by faith and not by sight.
His presence brings you to new levels and new heights!
God says, "Behold, I will do a new thing"
With great anticipation, allow it to come forth

Speak faith and live life –your dreams through Christ will be birthed.

PRAYER: Heavenly Father I thank You for placing Your dreams in my heart. I thank You that as I delight myself in You, that You will give me the desires of my heart. Father I thank You that I am committing all to You. Thank You Lord that You never give up on me and the plans You have for me, in Jesus' name, I pray. Amen!

DECLARATION: Through Christ, I can dream again. His dreams are manifesting in my life now!

*"And it shall come to pass afterward That I will pour out My Spirit on all flesh; Your sons and your daughters shall prophesy, Your old men shall dream dreams, Your young men shall see visions."* Joel 2:28

REFLECTIONS:

_____
_____
_____
_____
_____
_____
_____
_____

# BREAKTHROUGH

My breakthrough is here,
I will not fear.
My miraculous moment has arrived,
Through God's grace and mercy, I am alive.
I am more than a conqueror through Christ Jesus
And I proclaim if God be for us, who can be against us!
Nothing can separate me from His love.
In this moment, I realize I am justified,
In my life God is glorified.
His promises are manifesting in my life,
I am breaking through to the other side,
Nothing can hold me back not fear, nor pride.
This is my victory that overcomes the world,
even my faith,
I am breaking through by boldly coming
to the throne of grace.
The wait is over. It is finished!
I see it as God gives me a glimpse and I look ahead

It is so clear,
My breakthrough, now, it's here!

**PRAYER:** Heavenly Father I am so thankful that I am breaking through to the other side of my situation. By faith Lord, I am believing in Your promises and I thank You that I have my breakthrough in every area of my life. Please remove all doubt and unbelief as I embrace the answers to all that I have prayed for. I embrace this new season in my life, in Jesus' name. Amen!

**DECLARATION:** My breakthrough is here! It is my season. It is my time. God's promises are manifesting for me!

*"So David went to Baal Perazim, and David defeated them there; and he said, "The Lord has broken through my enemies before me, like a breakthrough of water." Therefore he called the name of that place [a]Baal Perazim."* 2 Samuel 5:20

**REFLECTIONS:**
_____
_____
_____
_____
_____

# BIOGRAPHY

Felicia Edmond resides in Maryland with her husband and children. She has been homeschooling her children for many years. She enjoys serving in her local church through leadership, Intercessory Prayer, teaching, and mentoring others. Mrs. Edmond enjoys serving and leading in various non-profit organizations. She has both a passion and a burden to see the body of Christ and others receive their breakthroughs and she enjoys seeing them experiencing the love of God. She has a Bachelor of Science in Accounting from Hampton University and a Master of Counseling from Trinity University. Mrs. Edmond enjoys reading and spending quality time with her family and friends.

www.ingramcontent.com/pod-product-compliance
Lightning Source LLC
Chambersburg PA
CBHW021121080526
44587CB00010B/590